Is It Big?

Seed
Learning

big

small

heavy

light

old

new

clean

dirty

Is it big?

Yes, it's big.

Is it small?

Yes, it's small.

Is it light?

No, it's heavy.

Is it old?

Yes, it's old.

Is it new?

Yes, it's new.

Is it clean?

No, it's dirty.

Let's learn about Japan.

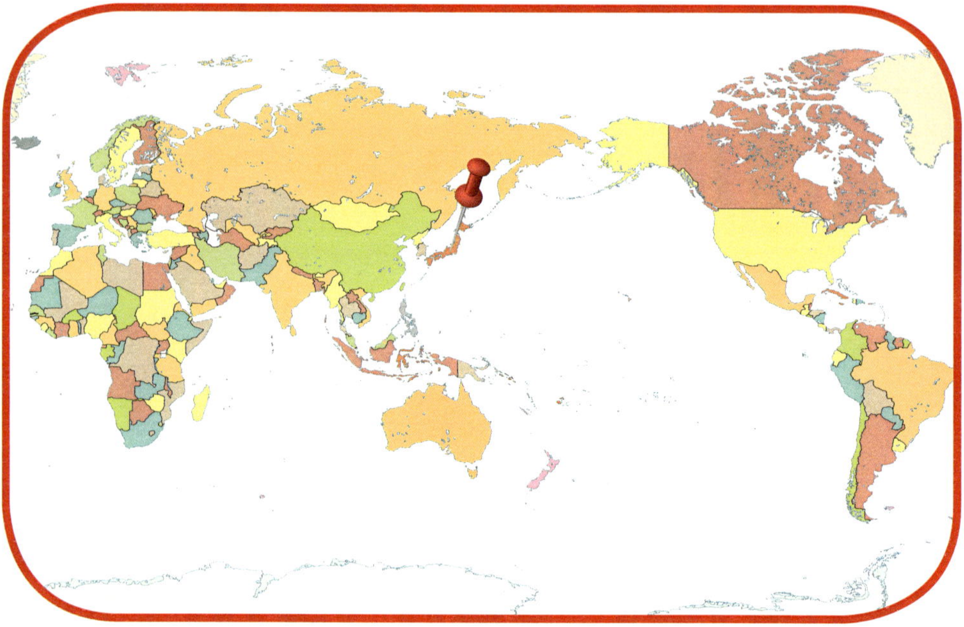

Flag of Japan

The Golden Pavilion